TRUE RESCUE
THE FINEST HOURS

The True Story of a Heroic Sea Rescue

Michael J. Tougias
and Casey Sherman

with illustrations by
Mark Edward Geyer

Christy Ottaviano Books

Henry Holt and Company • New York

Henry Holt and Company, *Publishers since 1866*

Henry Holt® is a registered trademark of Macmillan Publishing Group, LLC

120 Broadway, New York, NY 10271 • mackids.com

Text copyright © 2021 by Michael J. Tougias and Casey Sherman

Illustrations copyright © 2021 by Mark Edward Geyer

Library of Congress Cataloging-in-Publication Data is available.

ISBN 978-1-250-13753-1 (hardcover)

ISBN 978-1-250-13754-8 (paperback)

Our books may be purchased in bulk for promotional, educational, or
business use. Please contact your local bookseller or the Macmillan Corporate
and Premium Sales Department at (800) 221-7945 ext. 5442 or by email at
MacmillanSpecialMarkets@macmillan.com.

First edition, 2021 / Design by John Daly

Printed in the United States of America by LSC Communications,
Harrisonburg, Virginia

1   3   5   7   9   10   8   6   4   2 (hardcover)

1   3   5   7   9   10   8   6   4   2 (paperback)

CONTENTS

INTRODUCTION TO SHIPS, CAPTAINS, CREW, AND RESCUERS

On February 18, 1952, an incredible maritime event began when a ferocious nor'easter split in half a 503-foot-long T2 oil tanker, the *Pendleton*, approximately one mile off the coast of Cape Cod, Massachusetts. Here are the primary sailors and rescuers:

THE SAILORS ON THE *PENDLETON* STERN

GEORGE "TINY" MYERS.................COOK

CHARLES BRIDGES...................SEAMAN

RAYMOND SYBERT..........CHIEF ENGINEER

THE RESCUERS ON THE
36-FOOT MOTOR LIFEBOAT *CG 36500*

BERNIE WEBBER....................CAPTAIN

RICHARD LIVESEY..................SEAMAN

ANDY FITZGERALD.................ENGINEER

ERVIN MASKE..................CREW MEMBER

CHATHAM COAST GUARD STATION

DANIEL CLUFF..................COMMANDER

DONALD BANGS....................SKIPPER

CHAPTER ONE

THE *PENDLETON*

February 18, 1952

Captain John Fitzgerald could barely stay on his feet aboard his rocking ship, the 503-foot-long oil tanker named *Pendleton*. Fitzgerald had been in bad weather before, but nothing like the winter storm that was now raging off Cape Cod, Massachusetts. Fifty-foot waves battered his vessel violently in the predawn hours.

Suddenly a thunderous roar echoed through the bowels of the ship. The crew felt the gigantic tanker rise out of the turbulent ocean. This was followed by a shudder and an ear-splitting crash when the *Pendleton* nosed down seconds later.

Captain Fitzgerald wasn't sure exactly what had happened, but he knew by the sound that the ship had cracked. He immediately went to the radio set to issue an SOS, but the power had gone out.

Eighteen-year-old seaman Charles Bridges was asleep in his bunk when the ship tilted and cracked. He quickly grabbed a flashlight and ran to the top deck and then out on the catwalk leading to the bow. "Then I stopped in my tracks," remembered Bridges. "The catwalk floor disappeared. I realized just two more steps and I'd drop straight down into the ocean."

Bridges wheeled around and scurried to the mess deck, shouting, "We're in trouble! The ship has broke in two!"

Some of the men immediately wanted to lower the lifeboats. But Bridges told them that they were crazy, that the lifeboats wouldn't stand a chance in the enormous waves.

When the ship split in two, Captain Fitzgerald and seven other men were on the front section, called the bow. Their half of the ship now drifted away from the stern, the rear section, where the chief engineer, Raymond Sybert, and Charles Bridges huddled together.

George "Tiny" Myers, the ship's cook, tried to stay positive. He was a large man, weighing about 300 pounds. Usually he was singing or joking. But today he encouraged the men around him to be brave and work as a team. It

would be a big team, because a total of 33 men were on the stern.

The sailors on the back half of the ship knew the radio was in the bow. They also knew that once the ship split in two, the radio would be useless, because the ship's power came from the stern. That meant no emergency message could go out and the Coast Guard would not be aware of the disaster.

Sybert and Bridges nervously looked at each other, a feeling of hopelessness spreading over them. Bridges was thinking, *Who will come and save us?*

CHAPTER TWO

CHATHAM LIFEBOAT STATION

Bernie Webber stared out the window of Coast Guard's Chatham Lifeboat Station, on the "elbow" of Cape Cod. He watched snow and sleet whip the sand dunes and the ocean beyond. The 24-year-old boatswain's mate had already worked for many hours helping fishermen secure their boats to moorings in Chatham

Harbor. Now he was warming up with a cup of coffee.

No one at the station knew that the *Pendleton* had split in two. Incredibly, however, a second oil tanker—the *Fort Mercer*—had also cracked in half the same day. It was sinking not far from where the pieces of the *Pendleton* were drifting.

Over the marine radio Bernie listened to other Coast Guard men far out at sea. They were going to rescue the *Fort Mercer*.

Bernie thought of his good friend and life-boat skipper Donald Bangs. Just an hour earlier, Bangs had been ordered to take three more of their friends out on a 36-foot motor lifeboat to help the *Fort Mercer*.

When Bernie Webber heard the orders, he thought: *My God, do they really think a lifeboat and its crew could actually make it that far out to sea in this storm? They only have a compass to guide them.*

Webber figured that even if the crew didn't freeze to death, they would never be able to get the men off the storm-tossed sections of the *Mercer*. Bernie wondered if he'd ever see his friends alive again.

Webber's concern that the men might freeze to death was an all-too-real possibility. One of the human body's first responses to fight off hypothermia is to decrease the blood flow to the limbs. That helps reduce heat loss from the body's extremities, especially the feet and hands. Reduced blood flow to the limbs helps the body's efforts to keep the heart heated and beating. But the decreased blood flow to the hands, arms, and feet comes at a cost—the ability to perform tasks.

If the lifeboat's motor died, the men on board could not move their fingers to fix the problem. Hands and feet would also suffer frostbite. And in 1952, the gear they wore was quite basic, allowing them to become wet and cold.

Bernie was glad to be safe inside the Coast Guard station and not battling the 50-foot waves crashing on the open ocean. He had served in

the Coast Guard since he was 18. Although he was a quiet and humble young man, his courage and skills had already been tested many times in the unforgiving waters off the Cape.

Those waters were extremely dangerous because of shifting sandbars and enormous waves. In fact, seamen referred to the area as "the graveyard of the Atlantic," and for good reason. There are sunken skeletons from more than 3,000 shipwrecks scattered across the ocean floor from Chatham to Provincetown.

THE DECISION

Chatham Coast Guard Station Commander Daniel Cluff was in a different room than Bernie. He was closely examining two black dots on his radar screen. At first he thought they might be the two halves of the *Fort Mercer*. However, the objects were only a couple of miles from the shores of Chatham. *This is odd,* Cluff thought.

The Fort Mercer *is supposed to be thirty miles out to sea.*

Cluff called headquarters and asked a search plane to come and take a look. When the pilot arrived over the objects, he swooped down low. He could not believe what he saw. On the bow section of the ship were the letters *P-E-N-D-L-E-T-O-N*! It was not the *Fort Mercer* coming toward Chatham. The two floating pieces were an entirely different ship.

The pilot told Commander Cluff what he had discovered. Cluff was shocked. Now he had to order more of his men into action. Sailors' lives hung in the balance. Donald Bangs was the most experienced man at the station, but he was already at sea, pounding toward the *Fort Mercer*.

Cluff called Bangs on the radio: "There is

another oil tanker that has split in half," he told

the skipper. "It is the *Pendleton*. Both pieces are

drifting right toward Chatham. I want you to travel to the bow of that ship."

After Cluff gave Bangs the position of the bow, he knew he would have to send a different group of men to the stern. It was late afternoon, and it would be dark soon, but Cluff had no choice. The risks would be enormous, but someone from the station had to skipper a small boat to the *Pendleton*'s stern section before it was too late.

Commander Cluff walked over to the room where Bernie was sitting.

"Webber!" barked Cluff. "Pick yourself a crew. You got to take the *36500* out over the bar and assist that ship, ya hear?"

Bernie felt his heart drop to his feet. He could picture himself trying to steer the tiny wooden rescue boat over the hazardous Chatham Bar and into the high seas. This sandbar was a collection of ever-shifting shoals of sand only a few feet below the surface. When waves hit the bar, they became steep and their tops broke off, crashing with incredible force. These curling breakers were like the beach waves that knock people wading off their feet and send them tumbling. Now imagine one of those waves 60 feet high!

ALWAYS READY

The men on the *Pendleton* stern looked to Chief Engineer Raymond Sybert to take charge of that section of the ship. He was the highest-ranking officer now that Captain Fitzgerald had drifted away on the bow.

Sybert rallied the 32-man crew and ordered that all watertight doors be closed. He also assigned lookout watches at both ends of the boat deck. Then he went to observe the damage and saw that the *Pendleton* was spilling its load of home heating oil and kerosene into the sea. The thick black liquid covered the foamy crests of angry waves that rose and fell around the ship.

The *Pendleton* was a T2 tanker, a gigantic ship built to carry large supplies of oil. But some critics referred to them as "serial sinkers." The trouble with T2 tankers dated back nearly a decade, starting on January 17, 1943, when the *Schenectady* split in half while still at the dock!

Like the *Schenectady*, the *Pendleton* had been built quickly for the World War II effort. By all accounts, it looked sturdy enough. It weighed 10,448 tons and was powered by a turboelectric motor with a single propeller 11 feet wide. But the ship's strong-looking exterior concealed the subpar welding methods used in its construction.

After the *Pendleton* was torn in two, the waves carried both sections of the ship south

from Provincetown down the arm of Cape Cod. Because the tanker had watertight compartments in the cargo area, the halves initially stayed afloat.

One advantage the tanker had compared to the *Titanic* was the way it split in half. With the *Titanic*, an iceberg had ripped a long gash through the side of the ship, opening several compartments. But the *Pendleton*'s break was across its middle, damaging fewer compartments than if it had been ripped lengthwise across its hull.

The two sections of the *Pendleton* drifted all day long until they were only a mile or so from Chatham's Coast Guard station. So far, they had stayed afloat, but there was no way to know for how much longer. Tiny Myers, Raymond Sybert, and Charles Bridges grew even more concerned. And now it was getting dark as night approached.

Back at the station, Bernie was stunned that Commander Cluff was sending him out in a 36-foot rescue boat. Not only was it getting dark, but the more experienced crew had gone out earlier with Donald Bangs.

Bernie recalled the Coast Guard's official motto: *Semper Paratus*, Latin for "Always Ready." However, it was the unofficial Coast Guard motto that now weighed heavily in his mind: *You have to go out, but you do not have to come back.*

BERNIE AND HIS CREW

After Cluff told him to go out to the *Pendleton*'s stern, Bernie Webber stood at attention. "Yes, Mr. Cluff," Webber replied. "I'll get ready."

Then Bernie turned to the other men in the room and asked, "Who'll come with me?"

Richard Livesey was more than a little concerned. He had seen the mighty waves crashing over North Beach and knew this mission would be horrendous. Still, he fought the fear, fatigue, and cold running through his body and raised his hand. "Bernie, I'll go with you," he said.

Andy Fitzgerald (no relation to Captain John Fitzgerald) was also in the room and said, "I'll go." Andy had been bored all day and was eager to volunteer.

The crew still needed a fourth man. Ervin Maske was in the mess hall when he heard Webber's call. Maske was a guest at the station and could have easily said no to the mission. The 23-year-old from Marinette, Wisconsin, was a member of the Stonehorse Lightship. He had just returned from leave and was awaiting transport back to his ship.

Like Webber, Maske had a wife waiting for him at home. Ervin Maske had much to lose, and not much to gain, on this operation with a crew he had never met before. Still, he volunteered for the rescue mission without hesitating. Webber shook Maske's hand and told him to prepare.

The crew of four was ready and willing, but were they able? Webber, at just 24, was the oldest of the group and the most experienced.

Maske, Webber, Fitzgerald, and Livesey had never trained as a unit. In fact, the three crewmen from Chatham had never even met Maske until that very day. But the foursome had as many similarities as they had differences. All were in great physical shape, and all had joined the Coast Guard to save lives. Now was their chance.

Webber was the tallest, at six foot two, with a

lanky build and a reserved personality. Livesey, about four inches shorter, had a positive outlook with a good sense of humor. Andy, just short of six feet tall, had a ready smile and made friends wherever he went. Maske, the shortest of the group, was a relatively quiet young man. All four felt terrified of the violent ocean, but each mustered the determination to do what had to be done.

THE *36500*

With great trepidation, Webber, Livesey, Fitzgerald, and Maske departed the Chatham Lifeboat Station and drove to the Chatham Fish Pier. Webber parked the Dodge truck and stepped out into the snow. Through the thick snowflakes, the crew could barely see the small wooden lifeboat they would be taking on their journey. It was rocking back and forth in the distance.

The Coast Guard men walked to the side of the pier and climbed down a ladder and into a small boat called a dory. They were getting it ready to row out to the lifeboat when Webber heard a voice calling from the pier above them.

"You guys better get lost before you get too far out," cried a local fisherman. It was his way of saying, *Turn back while you still can.*

"Call Miriam and tell her what's going on!" Webber shouted back.

Bernie Webber had not spoken to his wife in two days. He thought of her home sick in bed, and his heart ached. Webber looked into the faces of the three other men in the dory, wondering how they'd hold up in the hours to come. He thought back to his wife again and wondered how she would cope if he didn't make it back.

As the crew rowed out into the harbor, Webber sized up the *CG 36500*. Like all lifeboats of its shape and size, the *36500* had been built at the Coast Guard Yard in Curtis Bay, Maryland. It was 36 feet, 8 inches long, with a 10-foot beam and a 3-foot draft. The boat weighed a solid 20,000 pounds. But Bernie wondered whether its builders had ever imagined a winter hurricane like the one that was now pounding the coast of New England.

Webber and his crew finally reached the *CG 36500* and climbed aboard. Webber, Fitzgerald, and Livesey were all familiar with the *36500*. Webber took his position in the wheelman's shelter. The crew departed the Chatham Fish Pier at 5:55 p.m. The sky had gone from charcoal gray to pitch black. The lights onshore grew smaller as the four men made their way across Chatham Harbor.

The crew could see the waves breaking on North Beach. Each man was now weighing the possibilities of how to get over the Chatham Bar. Webber wrapped a long leather belt around his waist and fastened himself to the wheelman's shelter. This would tie him to the vessel no matter how hard the waves hit it.

The *CG 36500* made a turn in the channel, where the men were met by the sweeping beam of Chatham Lighthouse. In the distance, Webber could see the dim lights glowing in the main building. *What's going on in there?* For a moment, he prayed that he would get a call on the radio ordering him to turn back. Webber grabbed the radio and called the station, giving Commander Cluff an update, hoping for a change in orders.

"Proceed as directed," Cluff responded with his Virginia twang.

There was no way to back out now.

CHAPTER SEVEN

THE CHATHAM BAR

Webber and crew pushed on. They were already fighting the severe cold. Their tired feet felt like blocks of ice inside their rubber overshoes. Reaching the end of Chatham Harbor, the men heard the roaring at the sandbar. Crashing waves created acres of yellowish-white foam.

This is not going to be a good trip, Richard

Livesey thought to himself. Livesey had the clear feeling he was living his last minutes on earth.

Andy Fitzgerald, who manned the searchlight mounted on the forward turtleback compartment, also felt trepidation. He was putting his faith in Bernie's experience and in the construction of the *36500*. Andy had always thought of the lifeboat as a floating tank—slow but very steady no matter what the weather.

As they motored forward, the searchlight partially illuminated the shoals of the bar. All four men caught a glimpse of what was ahead. Webber could not believe the height of the seas. His boat seemed smaller than ever. Scared and nearly freezing to death, Webber was now forced to make a decision that could very well cost the lives of his crewmen. *Do I turn back? Do I go ahead? What do I do now?*

Webber knew that he would not be criticized for turning back. Why add to the tragedy by sending four more men to their deaths on Chatham Bar? He cleared his head and turned his thoughts to the men he was attempting to save. They needed him, and he would not turn back.

As the lifeboat pitched along a canyon of waves, Webber and his crew spontaneously began to sing. They sang out of a mix of determination and fear. Their four voices formed a harmony that rose over the howling winds.

The singing subsided and the men grew silent as Webber motored the *CG 36500* into the bar. The searchlight cut through the snow and darkness. Andy could see—and feel—that the waves were growing and swirling from every direction.

He braced himself for the collision he knew was coming.

When they hit the sandbar, the tiny wooden lifeboat cut into a mammoth 60-foot wave. The mountain of bone-chilling water lifted the vessel, tossing it into the air like a small toy. All the men were temporarily airborne.

The boat and the men came crashing back down on the hard surface of the sea. Suddenly, another huge wave struck. This time, a torrent of water washed over the crew, knocking them to the deck. The violent wave shattered the boat's windshield, sending sharp shards of glass into Webber's face and hair as he fell backward.

The wave had spun the *CG 36500* completely around, and its bow was now facing the shore. It was the most dangerous position for the boat and the crew. Webber pulled himself up off the deck and tried to steer the boat back into the seas. He brushed bits of glass off his face with one hand, the other gripped firmly on the steering wheel. With the windshield now broken, the sea spray came through into the wheelman's shelter.

The snow and sea spray were hitting Bernie's face so hard he could barely open his eyes. As he tried to get his bearings, he glanced down to where the boat's compass should have been. The compass—his only navigation tool—was gone, torn from its mount. He now had to rely on instinct alone.

Blindly, Webber pointed the boat back toward the next oncoming wave. When the wave hit, Livesey had the sensation that the little lifeboat was being consumed by the wall of salt water. He could feel that the boat was on its side. For one sickening second he wondered if it would right itself.

The wave freed the boat from its grip. Webber used every ounce of his strength and again straightened the vessel. He gave it throttle, advancing the boat a few more precious feet. Seconds later, another wave slammed into them, again sending the vessel careening at a 45-degree angle.

Webber managed to get the lifeboat back under control. Then, despite the loud crashing of the ocean, each man realized one sound was missing. The motor had died, and the next wave was about to hit!

CHAPTER EIGHT

CHATHAM MOBILIZES

News announcer Ed Semprini finished a long day in the broadcast booth at a Cape Cod radio station. He had just returned home when he received a call from fellow journalist Lou Howes.

"Don't bother sitting down for dinner," Howes advised his friend. "We've got a tanker that went down off Chatham." Before Semprini could respond, Howes added to the graveness of the situation. "There's not one tanker," he said. "There's two of them! I'm heading to the Chatham Lifeboat Station right now."

"How about giving me a ride?" Semprini asked. "I'll go down with you." Semprini hung up the phone and then called his sound engineer, Wes Stidstone. "Gather your equipment, and meet me in Chatham," Semprini told him. "I think we've got a big story on our hands."

Lou Howes pulled up in front of Semprini's home and honked. The horn and the engine seemed to be the only parts that worked in the battered old Chevrolet.

Semprini heard the blare of the horn and

trudged through the snow toward his ride. He climbed into the passenger side and rubbed his cold hands in front of the heater. He quickly realized the heater was broken. *This trip better be worth it,* the newsman thought to himself as the jalopy pulled away from his house and into the blinding snow.

While the blizzard wailed outside, Cape Codders stayed in their warm homes and huddled around the radio as news of the rescue missions began to spread. Those with short-wave radios could listen to the dramatic live dispatches between the Coast Guard station and the rescue crews.

If the rescue crews somehow made it back alive, they would be cold, hungry, and probably very sick. The call went out to the town clothier to gather up warm clothes. The local

Red Cross was also alerted. Ordinary people at home began cooking warm meals for the seamen in hopes they would return. The people of Chatham had been raised on the sea. They knew what needed to be done to help the stranded sailors.

CHAPTER NINE

"HE CAME TO THE SURFACE FLOATING"

Those aboard the 36-foot Coast Guard lifeboat sent out earlier that day, skippered by Donald Bangs, were involved in a terrifying mission of their own. As they headed toward the broken halves of the *Fort Mercer*, Bangs and his crew almost didn't survive the first few minutes of their journey. When they rounded Monomoy

Point, they were assaulted by a huge breaking sea.

The skipper thought that if he tried to maneuver the boat over the waves, it stood a good chance of having its bow go straight up and then over the stern, capsizing. He only had a second to make a decision, but he gunned the engine and forced his tiny craft to punch *through* the waves. When the crew came out the other side, they were completely airborne; then, free-falling, they slammed into the ocean below.

Bangs was trying to save the lives of the men on the crippled tanker, but he was also concerned about the lives of his own sailors. So far, his mission had been filled with danger and frustration. Then, having been sent out to aid the *Mercer*, he and his crew were told to turn around and look for the *Pendleton*. Others would continue the *Mercer* rescue.

The men on Bangs's boat had already suffered greatly. The open cockpit of the lifeboat had no heat, and the men were constantly getting soaked by breaking seas and foam sheared from the crest of waves. Snow and sleet still fell, and the crew's ears, fingers, and toes were numb from the cold.

Pounding through the seas back toward Chatham, Bangs saw the *Pendleton*'s bow, eerily riding the seas with its forward end pointed upward into the dark night. Blasting his signal horn, he hoped to see someone appear on deck. Bangs tried holding his lifeboat in one place, just downwind of the hulk, and he and his crew listened intently for the shouts of trapped sailors. But there was only the wind, and the bow appeared deserted.

Where are the crewmen? Bangs wondered. *Were they swept off the ship? Did they take to the lifeboats?* There were absolutely no clues. The broken bow appeared to be a ghost ship, wallowing in the heavy seas, ready to sink to the depths at any moment.

And so the freezing Bangs and his crew turned their vessel once more toward Chatham, thinking they could help locate the *Pendleton*'s stern. They were more than halfway to the stern when their radio crackled. There were survivors onboard the *Pendleton* bow after all!

Bangs raced back to the bow. This time he moved even closer to the hulk, and as the wave crests carried his small vessel upward, he and his men were almost at eye level with the deck of the broken ship. And that's when they saw a lone man on the starboard wing of the wheel-house.

"We saw a man standing on the bridge,"

recalled Bangs. "He was hollering at us, but we couldn't hear a word. The man was then seen to jump or fall into the sea. He came to the surface floating about a boat length and a half from us. Just as we were about to fish him out of the water, the biggest sea of the night broke over our deck."

The skipper used his searchlight to try to find the man in the turbulent ocean. Bangs spotted him yards away, floating motionless on his back. Then the man disappeared. The sea simply engulfed him, and his fight for life was over.

None of the other seven men known to be on the *Pendleton* bow, including the captain, ever appeared at the railing, fired a flare, or flashed a light. One sailor was later found dead, frozen like a block of ice, on the ship. The others were likely swept away before Bangs arrived.

CHAPTER TEN

LOSING ALL HOPE: ONBOARD THE *PENDLETON* STERN

Adrift now for nearly 14 hours, the men aboard the stern of the *Pendleton* still had food, water, and heat, but they were running low on hope. The rescue mission for the *Fort Mercer* was fully under way, but the *Pendleton* crew had yet to hear anything on the radio about their own plight.

Chief Engineer Raymond Sybert had now assumed the leadership role for the crew. He was frightened by the enormous responsibility, and by the growing feeling that he and his men would not make it back alive.

Determined to stay composed, Sybert ordered the crew to keep the crippled vessel as far off-shore as they could. The crew had also rigged up an around-the-clock whistle watch, since the stern was able to maintain some of its power. The survivors blew that whistle for 12 straight hours without any response.

The men had been under enormous psychological stress ever since the *Pendleton* had split. One crew member maintained his confidence, at least on the outside. Tiny Myers had spent much of the day lifting the crew's spirits and shooting off flares to mark the stern's position on shore. The 23-year-old seaman Rollo Kennison of Kalamazoo, Michigan, gushed that Tiny was "the greatest man on earth."

Myers shot off another flare and handed the flare gun to Kennison. "Keep that, kid," he said with a smile. "I want it as a souvenir when we get to shore."

Charles Bridges went out on deck, hoping to see a rescue boat. One of these trips nearly cost him his life. "The spray had frozen on the decks, and when a big swell hit the ship, I lost my footing and started sliding across the deck. There was no way I could stop myself. I could see that my last chance was to grab the ship's railing and that, if I didn't, I'd be swept right under it and overboard. Luckily I got a hold of it."

Bridges said his spirits were at their lowest about midafternoon. "That's when we hit a shoal and it stopped the drifting. Every time a wave slammed the ship, it pushed us over another inch. There was a big discussion about taking to the lifeboats. I said, 'You're crazy if you think I'm going in one of those. As long as this ship floats, I'm staying right here.' I knew that if we got in the lifeboats, we probably couldn't even get away from the ship. The waves would have crushed us against the hull."

CHAPTER ELEVEN

IT'S A GHOST SHIP

The rescuers' engine was dead, and the crew would be soon if they couldn't get the small *CG 36500* lifeboat moving again. The sturdy vessel had one flaw: the engine stalled if the boat rolled too much while it was under way.

Andy Fitzgerald began carefully making his way from the bow to the engine compartment located just in front of the wheelman's shelter. The *CG 36500* continued to rise and fall as Fitzgerald tried to keep a firm grip on the rails. Andy wondered how long he could last if he got thrown overboard. *Not very long, so don't get thrown over,* he thought to himself as he held on for survival.

He made it to the engine room and crawled into the small space, made even smaller by the wet, heavy clothes he had on. Once he was inside the compartment, another powerful sea wave slammed into the lifeboat, bouncing Fitzgerald around. Andy cried out as he was thrown like a rag doll against the red-hot engine. Despite suffering burns, bruises, and scrapes, Fitzgerald somehow managed to control the pain as he held down the priming lever and waited for the gasoline to begin flowing to the engine again.

Andy restarted the 90-horsepower motor, and as it kicked back to life, Bernie noticed a change in the seas. The waves were even more monstrous now, but they were also spread farther apart. This confirmed that Bernie and his crew had defied the odds. They had made it over the Chatham Bar.

The men were soaked from the bone-chilling ocean, but they hardly noticed with so much adrenaline pumping. While Webber clung to the wheel, Livesey, Fitzgerald, and Maske kept a tight grip on the rails. The three crewmen knew they were heading farther out to sea, and silently hoped that Bernie would keep making the right moves.

The storm grew stronger as they ventured out to where the cauldron of wind and snow intensified even more. Webber's only option was to ride the waves like a thunderous roller coaster. He let the *CG 36500*'s engine idle as they climbed slowly and steadily up the sea. The crew braced itself as the lifeboat ascended toward the wave's curled, frothing peak. Bernie gunned the engine to get them over the top of the wave and held on as the lifeboat raced down the other side at breakneck speed.

Webber was given plenty of room to maneuver the vessel and was not burdened by a life vest, which he had decided not to wear because it would hurt his ability to steer the boat at the Chatham Bar. The lifeboat may have been as durable as a tank, but it was difficult to steer. The snow and sea spray continued to pound against his chest, and Bernie now wished he'd worn the life jacket, if only to protect himself from the cold.

Like the men aboard the stern section of the *Pendleton*, the crew of the *CG 36500* prayed this would not be their last night on earth. Although Webber wouldn't admit it to his men, his hope was fading. Again, he thought of Miriam, who was sick in bed at home. Who would be the one to tell her that her husband would never return?

Bernie peered through the broken glass of the windshield and felt his heart jump. A mysterious dark shape was rising menacingly out of the surf. He slowed the lifeboat down almost to a stop. *There's something there,* he told himself. "Andy! Go to the bow and turn on the searchlight!" Webber hollered.

Fitzgerald followed the order. He moved carefully toward the forward cabin and flicked on the searchlight switch. A small beam of light was cast, illuminating the huge object that was

now less than 50 feet away. Had Webber gone any farther, he would have crashed into the hull of the *Pendleton* stern. The steel hulk was dark and ominous, with no apparent signs of life. *We're too late*, Bernie thought to himself. *It's a ghost ship.*

CHAPTER TWELVE

A BEAM OF LIGHT

Raymond Sybert fought back his darkest thoughts as he and 32 other men sat helplessly inside the stern section of the *Pendleton*. There was nothing left for the men to do but ride out the storm and wait for help to arrive. *If it arrives.*

The crew members had been standing watch all day, but there was still no sign of life in the turbulent swells beyond the fractured ship. The chief engineer must have also been concerned about the fate of the ship's captain and the other men trapped on the bow. Had they been rescued yet? Just then, the man on watch noticed something bobbing up and down in the rolling seas—a small light, headed their way. The light looked no bigger than a tiny pinprick in the inky blackness.

Bernie Webber motored the *CG 36500* in for a closer look as Andy Fitzgerald continued to run the searchlight up and across the width of the tanker. The beam of light flashed on a group of letters that formed the name *Pendleton* painted high up. The giant ship looked enormous and indestructible. *How could it have split in two?* Webber thought as he maneuvered his tiny lifeboat down the portside of the stern.

An eerie silence hung over the ship as the wide-eyed lifeboat crew inspected the wreck. The silence was then broken by groaning sounds as the rescuers arrived at the gaping hole that was once connected to the bow.

Webber steered away from the giant tunnel leading to the bowels of the ship and guided the lifeboat around the stern, where the crew was startled by something new. A string of lights glowed high up on the decks—the fractured stern had not lost power after all. In the twinkle of the lights, they could also see a tiny figure! They had not come for nothing.

But how would they get this man off the deck? The survivor would have to jump and risk being engulfed by the waves.

As the *CG 36500* crew contemplated the next course of action, the man on the high decks disappeared. *Where did he go?* Bernie asked himself. Suddenly the figure returned, and this time he was not alone.

Three additional men were with him, and more crew members kept coming. Within a minute, over two dozen survivors in orange life jackets lined the rails. All of them looked directly down at the little lifeboat trying to maintain position in the tumultuous seas.

Fred Brown, a seaman on the *Pendleton*, and Tiny Myers were standing side by side on the rail. Tiny turned to Fred and, pulling his wallet out of his trousers, said, "Take my wallet. I don't think I'll get through this one." Fred was taken aback by the comment, but he retorted, "You've got just as good a chance as I have." Brown took the wallet and stuck it right back in Tiny's pocket.

CHAPTER THIRTEEN

MISSION IMPOSSIBLE

At first, Bernie was overjoyed at seeing so many sailors alive, but he quickly came to a frightening realization. It would be impossible to fit all those men on the 36-foot lifeboat. The responsibility hit Webber like a tidal wave. *How are we going to save all these men? If I fail, what a tragedy this will be.*

Bernie saw a rope ladder with wooden steps—a Jacob's ladder—drop over the side of the *Pendleton*. In the next instant, the stranded seamen started coming down as fast as they could.

The first man down the ladder jumped and landed with a loud crash on the bow of the lifeboat. The others clung tightly to the ropes as the ladder swayed dangerously outward while the *Pendleton* rocked in the seas. Their screams echoed over swirling winds as they slammed back against the hull when the ship rolled in the opposite direction.

Bernie drove the lifeboat in toward them, trying to time the maneuver just right so that each survivor would land in his boat and not in the icy water. With the rolling seas, that proved to be an impossible task.

Some of the survivors leaped toward the lifeboat only to find themselves plunging into the frigid swells below. The *CG 36500* was fitted with a safety line wrapped around the shell of the boat. The soaked seamen eventually found their way to the surface and grabbed the rope for dear life. Fitzgerald, Maske, and Livesey took hold of the swimmers and hoisted them up.

Once the survivors were safely on board, Andy, Ervin, and Richard led them down into the forward cabin and herded them inside, but that small space filled up quickly. With the added weight, the *CG 36500* was now taking on too much water.

As captain, Bernie had to make a life-or-death decision. *Do we stop now, and try to get the men we already have safely back to shore?*

Or do we go for broke? Webber decided that no man would be left behind. "We all live, or we all die," he told his crew.

TINY MYERS

While the rescue was unfolding, the stern section of the *Pendleton* rolled deeply, scraping against the ocean floor. The crew of the *CG 36500* continued to bring aboard survivors, squeezing them in wherever they could.

Thirty-one survivors were now huddling on a vessel that was meant to carry only 12 people, including the crew. The engine compartment overflowed with human cargo. Two men were still on the *Pendleton*'s deck: Raymond Sybert, who as de facto captain of the stern would be the last man off, and Tiny Myers. Fitzgerald kept the searchlight on the burly man as he made his way slowly down the Jacob's ladder. Myers was shirtless now, having given much of his own clothing to warm up other members of the *Pendleton* crew.

At this point, the swells surrounding the ship had become even more violent. *Just two more, and we can get outta here*, Bernie thought.

Myers had made it halfway down the ladder when he suddenly slipped and fell deep into the ocean. He resurfaced seconds later, and the lifeboat crew tried frantically to pull him on board. "Come this way!" Andy yelled. Myers drifted over to the inboard side of the lifeboat and grabbed hold of the line. Richard Livesey then leaned far out and reached for Myers's hand. The move nearly cost Livesey his life.

Myers was so heavy and strong that he began to pull Richard down into the water. Ervin and Andy rushed over to help, grabbing hold of Livesey by the legs and waist to prevent him from being pulled overboard.

As they tried in vain to hoist Myers onto the boat, the large man was swallowed by an even larger wave and disappeared from sight. A collective gasp of horror could be heard on the lifeboat as the survivors watched their friend vanish.

Bernie put the lifeboat in reverse and maneuvered away from the side of the ship.

The *CG 36500* came around in a circle as Andy kept the spotlight shining on the cresting waves. They finally caught sight of Myers in the darkness.

Due to the angle of the ship, the three propeller blades were now sticking out of the water. The seas were picking up, and Webber knew that he'd have only one chance to save this man.

He steered the bow of the lifeboat toward Myers and then eased slowly ahead. At that moment, Webber felt the back of the boat rise up as a huge wave lifted the *CG 36500* and threw it against the tanker. The lifeboat was now out of control and rushing toward Myers. Webber could see the panic in his eyes.

Ervin Maske reached out and managed

to grab hold of the big man one more time. A second later, they felt the sudden impact of a huge collision as the bow of the lifeboat rammed Myers, driving his broken body into the side of the *Pendleton*.

CHAPTER FIFTEEN

THIRTY-SIX MEN IN A 36-FOOT BOAT

Bernie Webber had tried desperately to avoid Tiny Myers as the lifeboat shot forward. He even tried steering the *CG 36500* in reverse, but that only stalled the engine again. Ervin Maske was the last man to get ahold of Myers, and he paid a price for it. Maske's hands had been crushed in the collision, and he could feel the blood pumping in his fingertips, which were now beginning to swell.

There would be no way to recover Myers's body now. Webber tried to put the thought out of his mind, and he successfully maneuvered the boat back to the ladder, rescuing the last man down, Raymond Sybert.

Bernie knew his crowded lifeboat could sink at any moment. Drifting in the darkness and with no compass to guide them, Webber still had no idea exactly where they were. *If I can just put the sea behind me and jog along, we'll end up in Nantucket Sound and eventually on the shallow water somewhere on Cape Cod,* he tried to convince himself. Bernie then relayed his plans to the rest of the group on board.

"If the boat all of a sudden stops, hit the beach," he commanded. "Don't waste any time asking questions. Get off and help those who are hurt. Just get off as fast as you can."

Webber felt that if he could get the boat's bow as close as possible to the beach and keep the engine going, the men would have a chance to get safely ashore. The survivors understood the plan perfectly. "We're with you, Skipper!" a shout came out. A loud cheer followed from the *Pendleton* crew.

At least one member of the lifeboat crew was not so optimistic, however. "The worst time for me was when we were going back in," Richard Livesey recalled. His arms were pinned by the crush of men standing in the well deck in front of the broken windshield.

They were now back in brutal seas without the protection of the massive *Pendleton* stern. The *CG 36500* was weighed down as powerful waves continued to crash over its crowded deck. *When will this end?* Livesey asked himself. It felt like an eternity. The lifeboat was riding so low, it seemed like they were traveling in a submarine. *If she doesn't come up a bit more, I'm gonna drown right here in the boat,* Richard thought.

As the *CG 36500* motored on, the seas began to change. The waves were not as heavy, though they were more frequent. The boat moved through shallower waters now. But they certainly were not out of danger. They still had the Chatham Bar to navigate.

Webber was considering his options. His commander began shouting orders over the radio about what he should do next. Webber turned off the radio so he could think. Suddenly he noticed a flashing red light in the distance. Could it be a buoy? Could it be the aircraft warning signal from above the tall radio station towers? Bernie rubbed his tired, salt-burned eyes. One minute, the light seemed to be way over

their heads, and then suddenly it shifted below the lifeboat.

As they approached, Webber ordered the man closest to the boat's searchlight to turn it back on. The blinking red light was becoming clearer now. The crew quickly realized it was coming from the buoy inside the Chatham Bar leading to the entrance into Old Harbor. Bernie looked at the blinking light once more and then lifted his gaze to the stormy skies above. In his heart, he knew that he would bring everyone aboard safely back to shore.

CHAPTER SIXTEEN

CHEERS IN CHATHAM

The *CG 36500* was now on a course that would return its crew and the 32 *Pendleton* survivors to the Chatham Fish Pier. The crew still had to make it over the Chatham Bar, where they had nearly been killed hours earlier. This time the vessel would be traveling with the seas. As they approached the bar, the crew noticed that the crashing surf didn't seem to be as loud as it was before.

Webber gave the boat a little throttle and punched its nose through the foam, and they were over the bar. He then radioed the Chatham Lifeboat Station and told the operator his position. The stunned radio operator couldn't believe the *CG 36500* had actually made it back to Old Harbor.

The operator immediately sent a dispatch to the other Coast Guard vessels:

CG 36500 HAS 32 MEN ABOARD FROM THE STERN SECTION. ALL EXCEPT ONE MAN WHO IS ON THE WATER THAT THEY CANNOT GET. NO OTHER MEN ARE MISSING THAT THEY KNOW OF. THERE SHOULD BE ABOUT SIX MEN ON THE BOW SECTION.

News of the rescue reached the Fish Pier, where Chatham residents had been waiting anxiously. A wave of applause rippled across the pier as townspeople hugged and cried, eager to see the boat.

Tears were also flowing on board the *CG 36500*. Bernie heard the crying of men who had been stuffed in the lifeboat's tiny forward compartment. Despite calmer waters and what must have been intense feelings of claustrophobia, the survivors remained holed up in the cabin, refusing to come out until they had reached port.

For people on the pier, the small, sturdy lifeboat was now in sight. Photographer Dick Kelsey positioned his big camera and began photographing what would become some of the most famous images in Cape Cod history.

Kelsey captured the battered vessel on

film as it came in rubbing against the wooden pylons. He could see the faces of the frightened but thankful men peering through the boat's shattered windshield and out of every porthole.

At that moment, Bernie gazed up at the Fish Pier and saw over a hundred local residents. They were the men, women, and children of Chatham, and all appeared to be reaching out their hands to grab the boat's lines and reel them in.

Once the *CG 36500* was safely tied up to the pier, townspeople helped the shaken survivors off the boat. The vessel had been so weighed down that Richard Livesey felt it rise each time a man got off.

An exhausted Bernie Webber stood quietly at the vessel's stern, his elbow resting on top of the cockpit, his forearm supporting his head.

His mind was filled with the terrifying images of the past several hours and the bravery of his crew. He thought about Tiny Myers and the look in the man's eyes just seconds before he went under. He thought about the 32 survivors on board. And he thought about Miriam and how he would be returning to her after all.

CHAPTER SEVENTEEN

BACK AT CHATHAM STATION

Newsman Ed Semprini rushed to the Chatham Lifeboat Station, where he met up with his engineer, Wes Stidstone. Both men were wired for sound when the *Pendleton* survivors came dragging in. The seamen were met by the local physician, Dr. Carroll Keene, who knew right away that many of them were in a state of shock.

Semprini didn't have much time. He had to get the interviews done quickly so that they could drive back to the radio station in Yarmouth and broadcast live.

He put his microphone in nearly every tired man's face as the survivors warmed up on coffee and doughnuts. The accents befuddled the veteran newsman, who was himself still learning to understand how Cape Codders spoke.

"One survivor from Louisiana asked me if his family could hear him speaking live." Semprini explained that the interviews would later be aired coast to coast on the Mutual News Network. Every survivor Semprini interviewed that night could not say enough good things about Bernie Webber and his crew. "They called it a miracle," Semprini remembered with a smile.

Webber, meanwhile, had walked upstairs to his bunk at the Chatham Lifeboat Station, still shaken by the worst storm of his life. He bent down and kicked off his overshoes. He then called Miriam. "I'm fine, and I'll be in touch with you tomorrow," he explained.

Bernie made his way down to the galley, where he was met by Andy, Richard, and Ervin. They all nodded toward one another. No one had to say a word. They would leave that to Commander Daniel Cluff, who expressed congratulations and admitted that he didn't think he'd see any of them alive again.

Ed Semprini had been searching for Bernie and finally spotted him coming out of the galley. Webber had been called the true hero of the rescue, and the newsman understood why.

Bernie answered a few questions as clearly

as possible. He did not feel like a hero. He just felt lucky.

"I kept thinking, where am I gonna put these men, how am I gonna get them off?" Bernie recounted. "If I fail, what a tragic thing, how can I live this down if all these men get killed? The responsibility, you feel it. It is on your mind."

He had finished his cup of coffee and devoured his doughnut, but now all he wanted was sleep. He returned to his bunk and collapsed.

AFTER THE STORM

Bernie Webber rubbed the sleep out of his tired eyes and felt a dull pain in every joint of his body. Despite his exhaustion, he had not slept well. The aches reminded him of what had happened.

Bernie looked to the floor and thought he was dreaming. Dollar bills were scattered, and his dresser drawer was overflowing with cash. Not knowing what this meant, Webber quickly got dressed, scooped up all the money, and went downstairs. The survivors were lying down to rest everywhere.

Bernie took the money to Commander Cluff. "Where did all this cash come from?" he asked.

Cluff told him that the money was a gift collected by the *Pendleton* survivors who had managed to retrieve some of their belongings before abandoning ship. The funds were eventually used to buy a television set for the Chatham Station, a rare luxury in 1952.

But some others felt differently about Bernie; his commanders were angry that Webber had not followed orders during the rescue. Some ranking officers were even threatening the words "court martial," because Bernie had turned off his radio and ignored higher authority while on the return trip to Old Harbor.

Cluff promised Webber that he'd handle the fallout himself. As it happened, Cluff did not need to protect Bernie or any other crew member. Later that day, Rear Admiral H. G. Bradbury, commander of Coast Guard First District, sent out this priority wire:

HEARTY WELL DONE TO ALL CONCERNED WITH RESCUE OPERATIONS SS *PENDLETON*. TO BERNARD C. WEBBER BM1 IN CHARGE OF *CG 36500* AND CREW MEMBERS ANDREW J. FITZGERALD EN2, RICHARD P. LIVESEY SN, AND ERVIN E. MASKE SN.

The *Pendleton* survivors did not remain at the Chatham Lifeboat Station for very long, but they did get the opportunity to express their feelings to Webber and the crew. "I'll never forget you fellows," survivor Frank Fauteux said, shaking their hands. "God bless you, I mean it." Fred Brown, a "wiper" (maintenance worker), nodded in agreement.

Later that morning, they piled onto a bus bound for a hotel in Boston. Along the way, they had to pick up two other crew members, 51-year-old Aaron Posvell of Jacksonville, Florida, and Tiny Myers's close friend Rollo Kennison, both of whom had been treated for shock and immersion at Cape Cod Hospital in Hyannis. As the bus left the Chatham Station, the seamen drove past the wreckage of their ship glistening in the morning sun.

By now, news of the rescue had stretched well beyond the small village of Chatham. The front page of the *Boston Daily Globe* reported 32 SAVED OFF TANKERS. Eighteen men aboard the sinking stern section of the *Fort Mercer* were rescued after leaping from the tanker to a Coast Guard ship called *Acushnet*. Thirteen sailors trapped on the bow section of the *Fort Mercer* stayed on board as the broken vessel was safely towed to New York City.

CHAPTER NINETEEN

THE GOLD LIFESAVING MEDAL

In the months following the rescue, Bernie Webber and his crewmen found themselves riding a different wave, one of public adulation. This proved to be an equally difficult task for the young Coasties, many of whom never thought they would be famous.

Webber felt remorse not only for Tiny Myers

and the others who perished but also for those heroes who were not getting the attention and credit they deserved for their roles in the miraculous rescue operation. He wanted to make sure that his fellow crewmen received the same honors he did.

Bernie Webber reunited briefly with Andy Fitzgerald, Ervin Maske, and Richard Livesey in Washington, D.C., on May 14, 1952. They had traveled to the nation's capital to receive the Coast Guard's highest honor: the Gold Lifesaving Medal.

Bernie told his commanders that he would not accept the award unless his crew members received the prestigious medal also. His wish was granted.

The Gold Lifesaving Medal, one of the oldest traditions in the U.S. military, was first awarded in 1876. The award can be granted to any member of the U.S. military who conducts a rescue within U.S. waters or those waters subject to U.S. jurisdiction. The Gold Lifesaving Medal is meant for those who attempt a rescue at "extreme peril and risk of life." And that is what Bernie, Richard, Andy, and Ervin did against all odds.

[Orleans Historical Society]

The *CG 36500* is the rescue boat Bernie and his crew took into the storm.

[Kelsey Photo]

The crew of the *CG 36500* spent hours battling the storm, searching for survivors. From left to right: Bernie Webber, Richard Livesey, and Andy Fitzgerald (Ervin Maske not pictured).

The crew of the *CG 36500* returns to Chatham pier as onlookers wait anxiously.

The bow section of the *Pendleton* after it split in half.

The men of the *CG 36500*, exhausted but grateful to be safely back on dry land. From left to right: Bernie Webber, Andy Fitzgerald, Richard Livesey, Ervin Maske.

When I first learned of the rescue of the *Pendleton* and the *Fort Mercer*, I was amazed at the courage of the Coast Guard men. I was also surprised that I had never heard of this event before. That is why I decided to write this book with Casey Sherman. Bernie Webber, Richard Livesey, Andy Fitzgerald, and Ervin Maske all risked their lives to save sailors who might have otherwise perished. Although Ervin Maske had passed away by the time I interviewed the crew, I did discuss the rescue with the other three men. They were so humble, insisting they were just doing their job. But I always thought they did their job and so much more.

—*Michael J. Tougias*

I grew up on Cape Cod and yet had never heard about this rescue. That is because Bernie, Richard, Ervin, and Andy never boasted about it to anyone. As a journalist, I was fortunate to have interviewed three of these brave men, as well as the family of Ervin Maske, and also newsman Ed Semprini. I feel that the lifeboat crew must be remembered for their selfless and courageous acts. To me, they are true superheroes. After Bernie Webber passed away, my mission was to get a movie made about the rescue. I knocked on a lot of doors until the great folks at Disney agreed to adapt *The Finest Hours* for the big screen. My favorite memory of that experience was the day that Disneyland held a parade in Andy Fitzgerald's honor before the movie premiere in 2016. It was great to see him and the other heroes recognized that way.

—*Casey Sherman*

GLOSSARY

BEAM: The width of a vessel at the widest part.

BOATSWAIN: The person in charge of the crew and equipment.

BOW: The front of a vessel.

BRIDGE: A room or elevated area where a ship can be commanded, usually the part of the ship where the navigation equipment is located.

DORY: A small boat with high sides and small bottom, often operated by oars.

DRAFT: The minimum depth a vessel can safely navigate. It is the distance from the bottom of the vessel to the waterline.

HULL: The watertight structure of a vessel.

NOR'EASTER: A storm along the east coast of North America, with winds coming out of the northeast. The term usually refers to a winter storm rather than a warm weather storm.

PORT: The left side of a vessel.

STARBOARD: The right side of a vessel.

STERN: The back of a vessel.

WHEELMAN'S SHELTER: Where the skipper, Bernie Webber, was steering the boat. He was looking through small glass windows.

ABOUT THE
AUTHORS AND ILLUSTRATOR

MICHAEL J. TOUGIAS is the author of many true rescue stories for young readers and adults, including the *New York Times*–bestselling adaptation *The Finest Hours: The True Story of a Heroic Sea Rescue*; *A Storm Too Soon: A Remarkable True Survival Story in 80-Foot Seas*; and *Into the Blizzard: Heroism at Sea During the Great Blizzard of 1978*. A frequent lecturer at schools, colleges, and libraries, Tougias divides his time between Massachusetts and Florida.

michaeltougias.com

CASEY SHERMAN is the *New York Times*–bestselling author of 11 books, including *The Finest Hours: The True Story of a Heroic Rescue at Sea*; *The Ice Bucket Challenge*; *12: The Inside Story of Tom Brady's Fight for Redemption*;

Above & Beyond; and *Boston Strong*. He frequently travels throughout the country to speak about his work and is represented by APB Speakers Bureau. He lives in Massachusetts.

MARK EDWARD GEYER is the illustrator of three Stephen King novels, including *The Green Mile*, as well as *Blood Communion* by Anne Rice, among other books.

markedwardgeyer.com

Research for *The Finest Hours* included government agency reports; interviews; books; and newspaper, radio, and magazine articles.

If you love the action in the True Rescue illustrated chapter book series and are looking for more in-depth coverage, don't miss these middle-grade true survival stories by Michael J. Tougias.

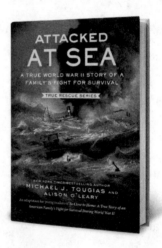